Note to Librarians, Teachers, and Parents:

Blastoff! Readers are carefully developed by literacy experts and combine standards-based content with developmentally appropriate text.

Level 1 provides the most support through repetition of high-frequency words, light text, predictable sentence patterns, and strong visual support.

Level 2 offers early readers a bit more challenge through varied simple sentences, increased text load, and less repetition of high-frequency words.

Level 3 advances early-fluent readers toward fluency through increased text and concept load, less reliance on visuals, longer sentences, and more literary language.

Level 4 builds reading stamina by providing more text per page, increased use of punctuation, greater variation in sentence patterns, and increasingly challenging vocabulary.

Level 5 encourages children to move from "learning to read" to "reading to learn" by providing even more text, varied writing styles, and less familiar topics.

Whichever book is right for your reader, Blastoff! Readers are the perfect books to build confidence and encourage a love of reading that will last a lifetime!

This edition first published in 2020 by Bellwether Media, Inc.

No part of this publication may be reproduced in whole or in part without written permission of the publisher. For information regarding permission, write to Bellwether Media, Inc., Attention: Permissions Department, 6012 Blue Circle Drive, Minnetonka, MN 55343.

Library of Congress Cataloging-in-Publication Data

Names: Albertson, Al, author.
Title: Black Bears / by Al Albertson.
Description: Minneapolis, MN : Bellwether Media, Inc., 2020. | Series: Blastoff! readers: animals of the forest | Includes bibliographical references and index. | Audience: Ages 5-8 | Audience: Grades K-1 | Summary: "Relevant images match informative text in this introduction to black bears. Intended for students in kindergarten through third grade"-- Provided by publisher.
Identifiers: LCCN 2019024607 (print) | LCCN 2019024608 (ebook) | ISBN 9781644871256 (library binding) | ISBN 9781618918017 (ebook)
Subjects: LCSH: Black bear–Juvenile literature.
Classification: LCC QL737.C27 A43 2020 (print) | LCC QL737.C27 (ebook) | DDC 599.78/5--dc23
LC record available at https://lccn.loc.gov/2019024607
LC ebook record available at https://lccn.loc.gov/2019024608

Text copyright © 2020 by Bellwether Media, Inc. BLASTOFF! READERS and associated logos are trademarks and/or registered trademarks of Bellwether Media, Inc.

Editor: Betsy Rathburn   Designer: Josh Brink

Printed in the United States of America, North Mankato, MN.

Table of Contents

Life in the Forest	4
Season of Sleep	10
Feasting in the Forest	16
Glossary	22
To Learn More	23
Index	24

Life in the Forest

American black bear

Black bears are **mammals** that live in the forest **biome**.

Many black bears live in parts of North America. Others live in Asia.

American Black Bear Range

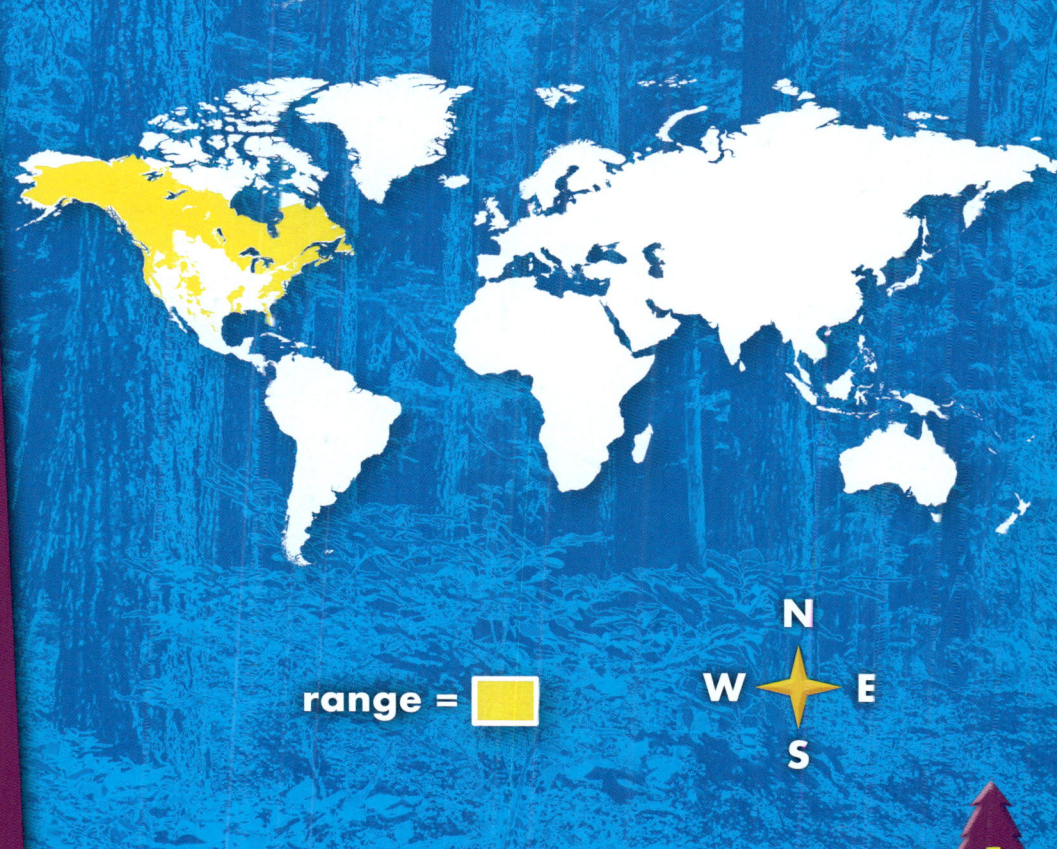

range =

N W E S

guard hairs

Forests can have cold winters. Two layers of fur keep black bears warm.

Long **guard hairs** cover soft, thick **underfur**.

Asiatic black bear

Forests are filled with food. Black bears use **curved** claws to find meals.

Special Adaptations

curved claws

two layers of fur

strong legs

The bears climb tall trees to reach nuts. Their claws turn over rocks to find **insects**.

9

Season of Sleep

Forest winters can be tough. It is hard to find food in cold weather.

Many black bears stay **dormant** in **dens** until spring.

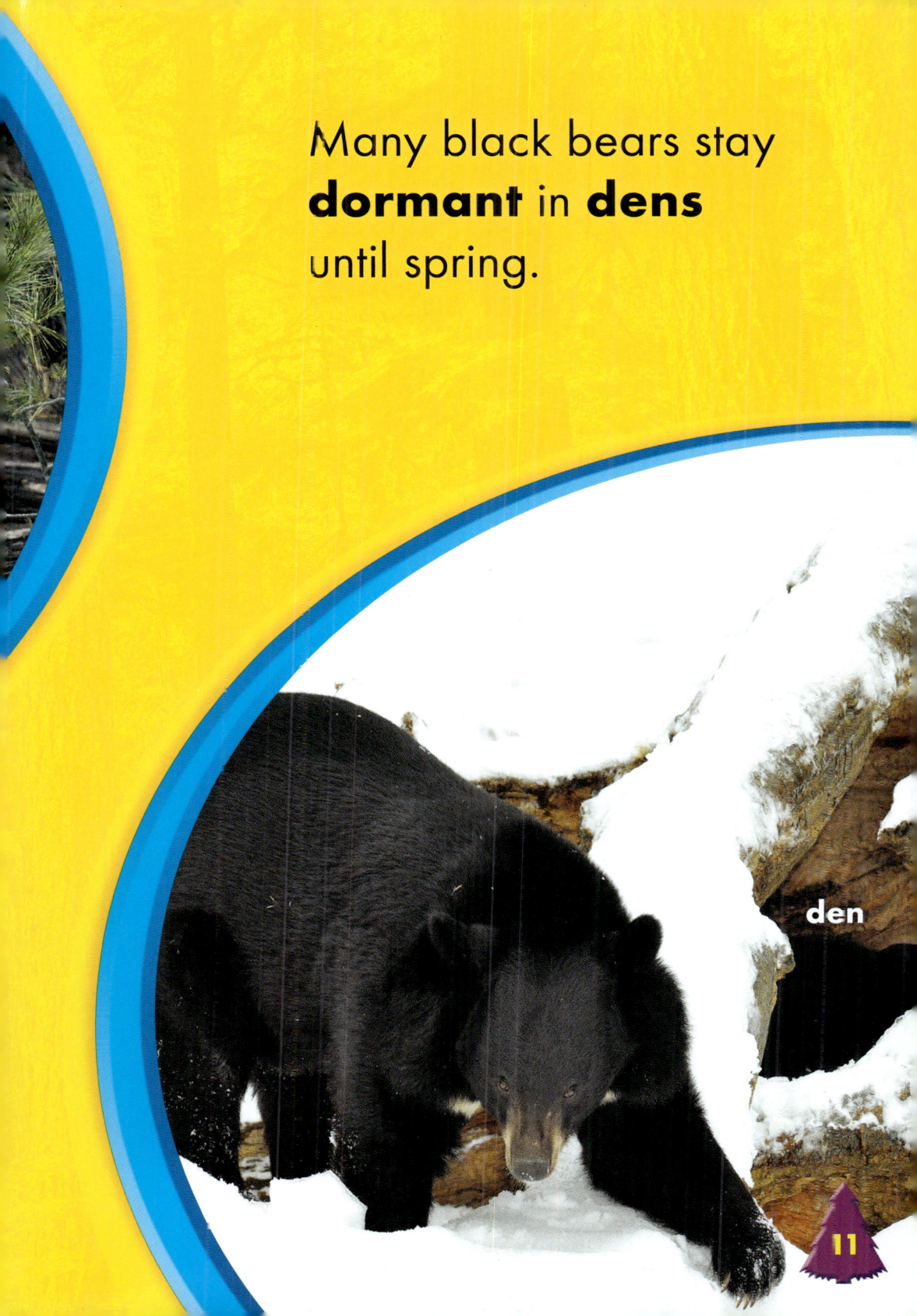

den

Forests have many places to sleep. The bears make dens in trees or caves!

In spring, females give birth to **cubs** in their dens. These homes keep black bears safe!

dormant female with cubs

Black bears travel alone. Strong memories guide them through large **ranges**.

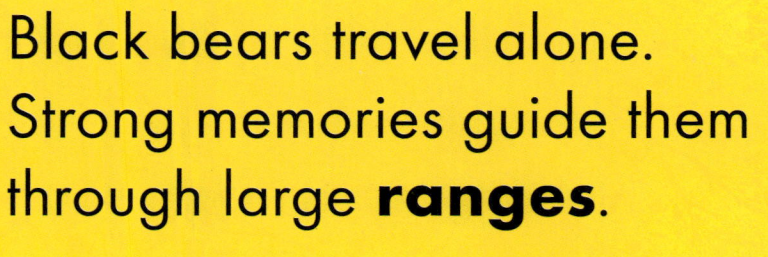

The bears do not mind sharing their range. If they run into danger, black bears run away!

Feasting in the Forest

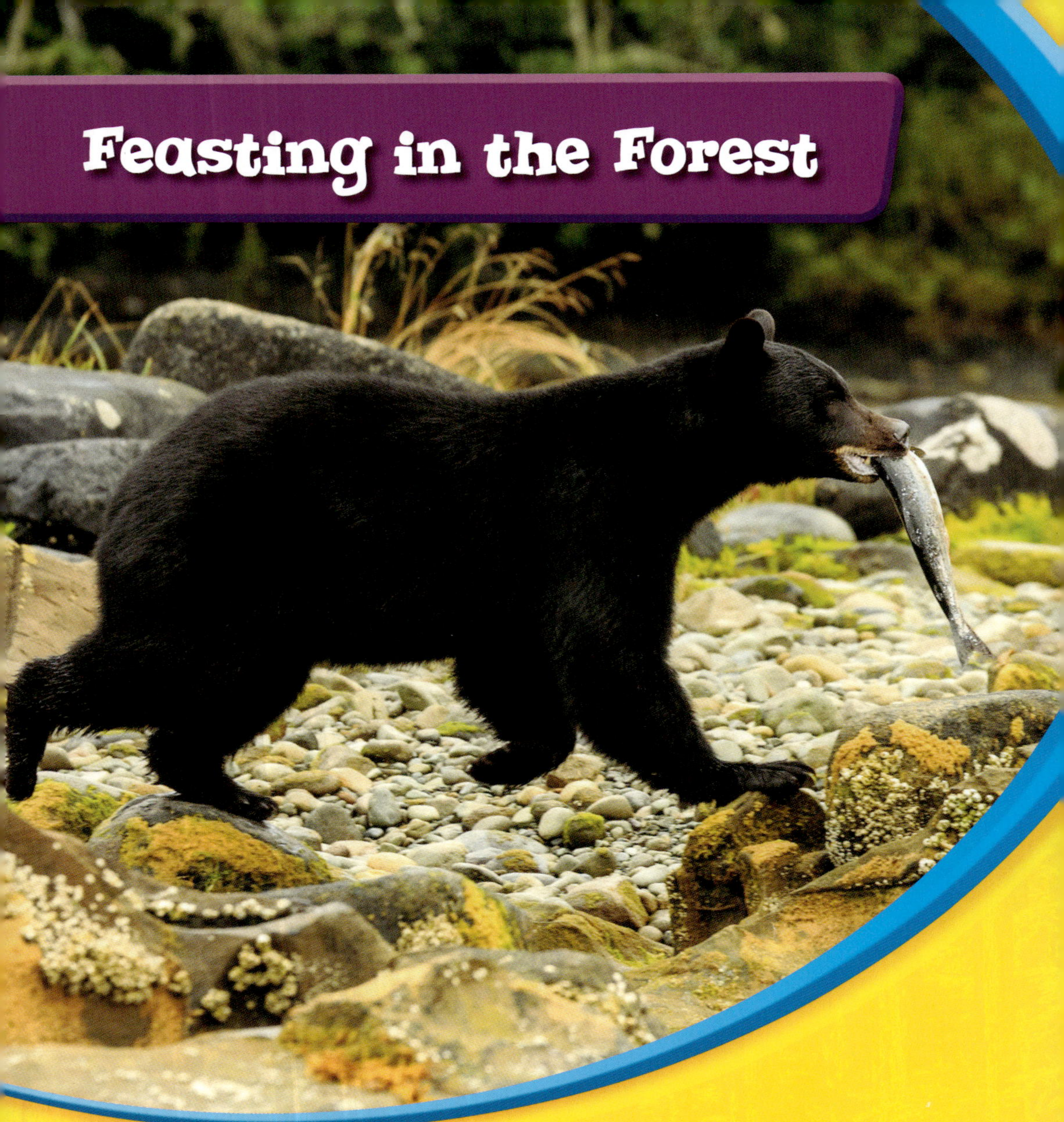

Black bears are **omnivores**. They enjoy grasses and berries. They also eat fish.

Their strong sense of smell helps sniff out tasty foods.

Long lips help black bears pull berries from branches.

Black Bear Diet

dandelions

blueberries

red salmon

Their long, thin tongues easily reach bugs in fallen logs!

Black bears can eat a lot of food every day.

The forest biome offers a big menu for these hungry bears!

American Black Bear Stats

Least Concern	Near Threatened	Vulnerable	Endangered	Critically Endangered	Extinct in the Wild	Extinct

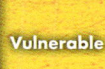

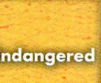

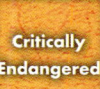

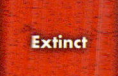

conservation status: least concern

life span: up to 20 years

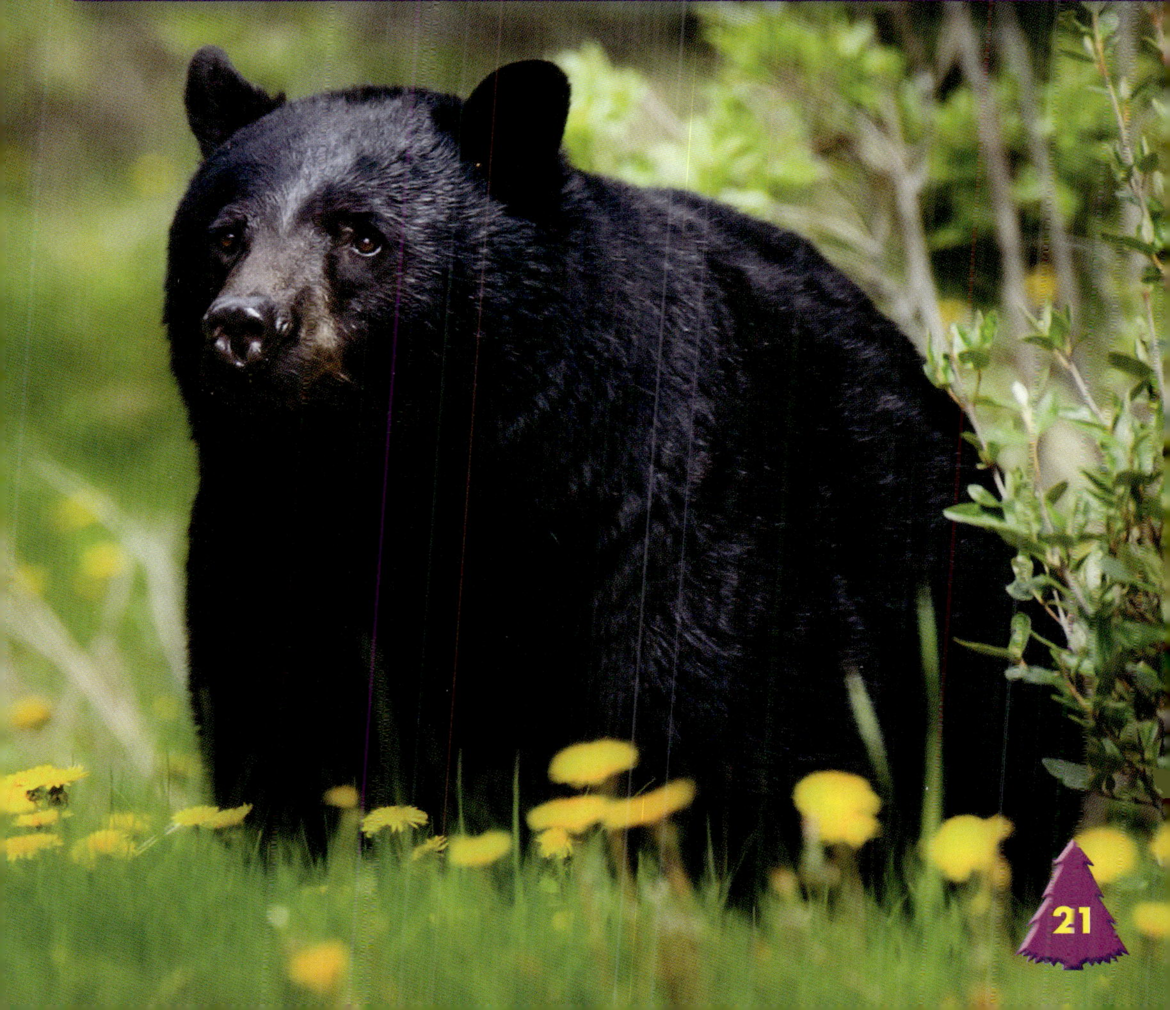

Glossary

biome—a large area with certain plants, animals, and weather

cubs—baby black bears

curved—curled or rounded

dens—sheltered places

dormant—not active

guard hairs—long, thick hairs on the outside of a black bear's coat

insects—small animals with six legs and hard outer bodies; an insect's body is divided into three parts.

mammals—warm-blooded animals that have backbones and feed their young milk

omnivores—animals that eat both plants and animals

ranges—the areas where black bears live

underfur—an inner layer of short, soft hair that keeps black bears warm

To Learn More

AT THE LIBRARY

Gleisner, Jenna Lee. *Black Bears*. Minneapolis, Minn.: Jump!, 2019.

Omoth, Tyler. *American Black Bears*. Lake Elmo, Minn.: Focus Readers, 2016.

Petrillo, Lisa. *All About North American Black Bears*. Hallandale, Fla.: Mitchell Lane Publishers, 2019.

ON THE WEB

FACTSURFER

Factsurfer.com gives you a safe, fun way to find more information.

1. Go to www.factsurfer.com.

2. Enter "black bears" into the search box and click 🔍

3. Select your book cover to see a list of related web sites.

Index

adaptations, 9
Asia, 5
biome, 4, 20
claws, 8, 9
climb, 9
cubs, 12
danger, 15
dens, 11, 12
dormant, 11, 12
females, 12
food, 8, 9, 10, 16, 17, 18, 19, 20
fur, 6, 9
guard hairs, 6, 7
legs, 9
lips, 18
mammals, 4
memories, 14

North America, 5
omnivores, 16
range, 5, 14, 15
smell, 17
spring, 11, 12
status, 21
tongues, 19
travel, 14
underfur, 7
winters, 6, 10

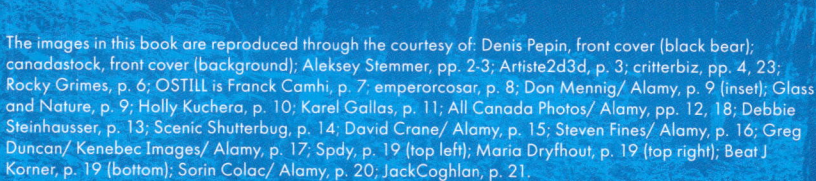

The images in this book are reproduced through the courtesy of: Denis Pepin, front cover (black bear); canadastock, front cover (background); Aleksey Stemmer, pp. 2-3; Artiste2d3d, p. 3; critterbiz, pp. 4, 23; Rocky Grimes, p. 6; OSTILL is Franck Camhi, p. 7; emperorcosar, p. 8; Don Mennig/ Alamy, p. 9 (inset); Glass and Nature, p. 9; Holly Kuchera, p. 10; Karel Gallas, p. 11; All Canada Photos/ Alamy, pp. 12, 18; Debbie Steinhausser, p. 13; Scenic Shutterbug, p. 14; David Crane/ Alamy, p. 15; Steven Fines/ Alamy, p. 16; Greg Duncan/ Kenebec Images/ Alamy, p. 17; Spdy, p. 19 (top left); Maria Dryfhout, p. 19 (top right); Beat J Korner, p. 19 (bottom); Sorin Colac/ Alamy, p. 20; JackCoghlan, p. 21.